Prince Edward Island

Photography by Sherman Hines
Introduction by David MacDonald

NIMBUS PUBLISHING LIMITED

Nimbus Publishing Limited
P.O. Box 9301, Station A
Halifax, Nova Scotia,
B3K 5N5

Design by Graphic Design Associates,
Halifax, Nova Scotia
Printed in Hong Kong by
Everbest Printing Co., Ltd.

Captions researched and written by
Julie V. Watson

Canadian Cataloguing in Publication Data

Hines, Sherman, 1941-
Prince Edward Island
ISBN 0-920852-39-4.
1. Prince Edward Island - Description and travel - 1950- Views. I. Title.
FC2612.H55 1985 917.17'0022'2 C85-098087-9
F1047.8.H55 1985

Introduction

"The fairest land 'tis possible to see"
Jacques Cartier on first sighting P.E.I. in 1534.

These photographic glimpses by Sherman Hines are vivid proof that not that much has changed over the last 450 years. Prince Edward Island has seen many people "come from away" to explore its beaches, harbours, grassy meadows, gentle slopes and brooks. While some like Cartier, Champlain, Cabot and Wolfe rested only briefly, others have made their home here for centuries.

Our original people, the Micmacs, called their island *Abegweit* — "Cradled on the Waves". According to legend, their great god, Glooscap, who had just completed painting the beauties of the world, concluded by taking his palette, a mixture of all the earthly colours and created from it "The Island". Colours in all their abundance there are, not harsh or garish, but soft and subtle. One senses an understatement of life that is present in land and people.

The Micmacs were joined in the 17th century by French settlers who named it Isle St. Jean in honour of their patron saint. For the next century and a half, it remained a colony of France, but war with the British meant loss of their island home and expulsion of almost all the French inhabitants. Miraculously, those few who tenaciously survived remained to become the ancestors to a significant number of the present island population. The new landlords, the British, on the eve of the 19th century declared this to be Prince Edward Island. To honour the Duke of Kent and future father to Queen Victoria. Immediately they set about to encourage their own immigration. Enterprising landholders and colonial entrepreneurs rounded up poor Scots and Irish with enticing stories of a promised land in the New World.

Throughout the 19th century these instant Islanders struggled to create a new life and home for themselves. In time, they gained both political and economic rights, and in addition, the island quickly became the centre of a booming shipbuilding industry which was among the largest in the world at that time. Island forests were rapidly consumed to create an ocean fleet carrying boatloads of lumber and fish to hungry European markets. By the end of the 19th century, the era of wooden ships and iron men had been replaced by iron vessels and steam. Small community industries had given way to large scale industrialization. This resulted in another great migration off the island. Tens of thousands of Islanders sought new opportunity elsewhere.

But Islanders have a way of returning, as do many others. Some have observed this homing quality. You perhaps have noted the unique red soil, which is attributed to the presence of large amounts of iron oxide. Could it be that so much iron creates a magnetic attraction for all who come near its shores? There is no doubt that whether you are Island-born or adopted, you will be constantly drawn by some mysterious, if not magnetic force, whether you are discovering "The Island" for the first or the one thousandth time. It is sure that though you may find it small, it is not simple. The passions and pleasures are as varied as harness racing to musical comedy. We take pride in our contribution to the building of the Nation itself, but most of all we are fascinated by a delicate landscape whose capacity for variation and change seems almost infinite.

David MacDonald,
Canadian Emergency Coordinator,
African Famine

Captions

1. Micmac legends tell how the Great Spirit created the Island from red clay, naming it "Minegoo — the most beautiful place on earth". Today the rich red clay is most in evidence on farm lands, unpaved roads and ploughed fields. The iron oxide, or rust, provides a beautiful colour-contrast to the red, green and blue of the fair Isle's landscape.

2. The waters of St. Peters Bay are dotted with rows of white floats used in aquaculture farming. This particular bay is used to farm Island Blue Mussels. Similar farming techniques are used to produce the renowned Malpeque Oysters.

3. Summerfield. Harvest turns flowing blankets of golden grain to symmetrical ribbons of straw drying in the warm Island sun.

4. Acres of fertile farm land surrounds tidy farm homes with a hint of the Victorian in their architecture.

5. The first settlers brought sheep to the Island. They were highly valued, particularly for their wool as all new clothing had to be hand produced. Today, sales of Island lamb, wool and breeding of purebred stock keep the industry healthy.
Horses dominate the landscape of the province, seeming to appear at every turn. Having the highest ratio of horses per person in the country has earned Prince Edward Island the nickname, "Kentucky of Canada".

6. Haymaking is of vital importance to farmers who rely on this source of feed for their livestock through the long winters. In days past hay was exported.

7. Upper Right - Decoy Carver, Winsloe;
Upper Left - Grain Farmer, Summerfield;
Lower Left - Reflecting On The Passing of Time;
Lower Right - Kitchen Witch Tea Room, Long River.

8. Mont Carmel: Much of the Island's heritage is being preserved in historic sites and museums, particularly by the P.E.I. Museum and Heritage Foundation and the Acadian society.

9. Potatoes are the most important cash crop on the Island accounting for a third to a half of the total farm receipts per year. Their dollar value can more than double the combined values of all other agriculture including grain, hay, cattle, pork and so on.

10. Early morning mists rising off rivers and bays give an ethereal charm to the countryside. A common occurrence when nights are cool and waters still hold the warmth of a summer sun.

11. Country homes welcome visitors to enjoy a rural vacation offering a perfect atmosphere to unwind... to just be yourself.

12. Maximeville: The official French Acadian Flag was chosen at Miscouche as part of the second National Acadian Convention in 1884. This distinctive flag is a symbol of cultural pride and is prominently displayed throughout Acadian Prince Edward Island. The yellow star represents the "Stella Maris", the star of the Virgin Mary, patron saint of the Acadian people.

13. St. Peters Bay Church, in the village of the same name, was built in 1881 of Island brick. Because of deterioration of the brick the church has now been restored and painted white, leaving only one church with the original brick. During a terrible fire many years ago, a 200-foot steeple toppled, burying its cross in six feet of earth in the churchyard. It remains there to this day, beside a lovely chestnut tree.

14. Most Island fishermen are equipped with day-boats which can be used for trapping lobsters, seining for herring, dragging for groundfish or scallops, taking paying passengers to jig for cod or mackerel or chasing the mighty tuna, all with a simple equipment change.

15. Sand Patterns - nature's own art form created by wind and swirling grasses in the dunes.

16. & 17. North Rustico Beach: Gathering "the Moss" along the coast... The seaweed, Irish Moss, is a cash crop free for the taking. This profitable seaplant is washed up close to the shore during gales, and as soon as weather permits, the shoreline is a flurry of activity as fishermen with trucks, tractors, carts and horses collect the moss. Piles of moss drying on wharves or roadsides are a common sight on the northshore. Moss is refined to produce carrageenin, used as a stabilizer in food processing, cosmetics, glazes, to name a few. It is a certainty that every Canadian uses moss daily.

18., 19., 20. Rustico Bay is one of the oldest established areas in the province. In 1735 a Norman peasant named René Rassicot began a fishing community at what is now Rustico Harbour. The name "Rustico" is an Anglicized corruption of his name. This colourful, working fishing port is a popular spot for those looking for a fishing trip or fresh seafood, particularly the most sought-after crustacean in the Maritimes, the lobster.

21. Aerial view near Charlottetown.

22. This aerial view shows the entrance to Rustico Bay, dominated by the breakwater jutting out into the Gulf of St. Lawrence at the top of the point of land. Court Brothers' Wharf on the opposite side of the land-end lures many youngsters to watch jellyfish, crabs, flounders and try their hand at fishing. The Court Family have been established at Rustico Harbour for over 100 years.

23. Wood Islands East: Typical of the country inns found in Prince Edward Island.

24. Anne of Green Gables is the most loved character in Canadian literature. Each year droves of visitors happily scour the Island for locations described in Lucy Maud Montgomery's books. The Cavendish house preserved as "Green Gables" was actually the home of cousins of the author. Its rooms correspond to those described in the "Anne" novels. Now maintained by Parks Canada, the house, walks and surrounding gardens enchant people from as far away as Japan.

25. Built in 1820 the Long River Old Mill is now a museum. The privately-owned collection provides a look into the past.

26. Harmony between land, sea and man... Lighthouses, familiar landmarks set among golden grain, seagrass or red Island clay, backed by a changeable ocean.

27. Sun breaking through the clouds marks the passing of a storm but pounding surf will serve as a reminder of its fury for hours to come.

28. St. Peters Harbour: Dockside serenity reveals little of the early dawn excitement when fishermen hastily organize equipment, crews and passengers for a day of deep-sea fishing.

29. Pastoral serenity on an overcast day.

30. Shingled frame farmhouses prevail as wood is the most available building material. They are usually painted snowy white with a coloured trim. Islanders nestled their homes in hollows or behind trees for protection against the harsh winds of winter.

31. Soaring shingled steeples were one of the architectural signatures of Island architect, William Critchlow Harris. No architect has left his mark more distinctly in the province.

32. Refreshing cool evenings of summer lure people to wharves such as this one in Stanley Bridge where they can savour the soothing sounds of water lapping against pilings and boats, the indescribable scent of the sea and the visual beauty of light cast over the water.

33. The thrifty Island nature at times means every square inch of land is cultivated leaving none for such flippancies as lawns.

34. & 35. Cavendish Beach: The Prince Edward Island National Park offers 40 kilometers of fabulous salt-water beaches. It is one of the most visited National Parks, attracting a million and a half visitors each year, yet a private spot can always be found for those who prefer solitude. The magnificent white sand dunes provide a stunning contrast to the clean blue ocean and red cliffs. During July and August warm waters prevail.

36. The Island is nearly 15 km from the nearest point on the mainland, Cape Tormentine, New Brunswick, making necessary the regular operation of ferries. The drive-on boats operate day and night, year round, with ice breakers keeping the crucial road link open in winter. Strangely, the Island serves as 'mainland' for a community even more isolated — the Magdalen Islands in the middle of the Gulf of St. Lawrence, which are served by a ferry out of Souris.

37. Olde Charlottetown, slowly being returned to its original glory and stature of importance by a restoration project, can be enjoyed by a walking tour or a leisurely horse and buggy ride, complete with a knowledgeable guide.

38. While government regulations call for standardized directional signs, several such as these have become an integral part of the landscape.

39. The strong cultural ties between the province and the British Isles are very evident at Woodleigh Replicas. Scale models of famous homes, castles and cathedrals of legendary, historical and literary interest are set in spacious grounds. The huge Tower of London (shown here) reigns over all in the Burlington attraction.

40. Charlottetown Driving Park: Harness racing is in the blood of most native sons and it's never long before newcomers catch the "bug" and head for the track. Whether on private tracks, ice, or larger raceways, sulkies head for the wire determined to set new trotting or pacing records. Year-round excitement culminates in prestigious races at the Summerside Lobster Carnival and Charlottetown's Old Home Week. Steps are now under way to open the Canadian Harness Racing Heritage Museum near the Charlottetown Driving Park.

41. Lily's Bakery, Bell River: Selling baked goods and handcrafted wares provides an extra summer income, much to the delight of the traveller.

42. In the shallows of ponds, bays and inlets Great Blue Herons stand absolutely motionless. Often more than 20 will be in the same area, indicating abundant schools of fish.

43. Receding tides leave behind a sampling of shells and seaweeds, here Island Blue Mussels and Irish Moss, to delight the beachcomber.

44. It's an anxious time for farmers — the hay is down and must be turned and turned again to dry in the summer sun before baling. Rain clouds can descend with little warning, destroying the nutritive value of this stable livestock feed.

45. Agriculture is P.E.I.'s most important primary industry. With the Island's rich red soil and moderate climate, it is no wonder that it has been given the nickname, "Canada's Million Acre Farm."

46. & 47. With a reliable ferry link to the mainland and an extensive network of paved roads, the trucker has become vital to the economy of the Island.

48. Reflecting rays of a setting sun create the image of a house filled with liquid gold.

49. Round bales weighing approximately half a ton, have replaced the smaller rectangular ones at a number of cattle operations.

50. Potatoes have been grown on the Island since the early days of French settlement when pioneers supplied produce for the garrison of Louisbourg, Cape Breton. Today both table stock and seed potatoes are exported around the world.

51. Once harvesting begins it continues late into the night. With modern technology it is possible to take "spuds" from the ground and have them in the warehouse in less than an hour. Equipment is expensive and often harvesting is done on contract with the danger of frost making time crucial to a successful crop.

52. Working farm near Belfast.

53. Between Lower Newton and Orwell Cove. Evening mists appear magically with the setting of the sun.

54. Islanders have learned to watch the animals, the sea and the sky to help them forecast the weather. One of the most reliable indicators are the clouds: fair weather pillow, mackerel sky or mare's tails, all help outdoor people plan their day.

55. Pinette South: Working in fields of shoulder-high tobacco, workers 'prime' the crop. Harvesting tobacco is a tedious job. Working between chest-high rows of the lush plants, workers remove lower leaves, leaving the top to continue growing.

56. At certain times there seem to be as many gulls in the fields as at the shore. Braving the dust churned up when a farmer cultivates his ground for seeding, they search for worms and insects — a change from shellfish and discarded fish.

57. Dairy farms such as this one in Pownal fulfill local needs in fluid and processed milk and supply processors of cheese, ice cream, butter and evaporated milk for export as well as home use.

58. Once grain is harvested a secondary crop, straw, is baled to use as a bedding for animals, strawberries and even to "bank" around houses to keep out the cold draughts of winter.

59. Mud Puddle Pottery, Mt. Mellick: The majority of the one-room schools have been abandoned by the education system. However, many have found a new use as studios and outlets for craftsmen who are forming an important Island industry.

60. North Rustico: Bargain seekers find yard sales of every description. Summer "visitors" bring along a bit of home to make a little cash on the side, selling handcrafts and other items.

61. With the majority of fishing boats following the same basic design many owners express their own individuality through the colours they paint their boats.

62. Glorious perfection in the heavens is given to us two-fold when perfectly mirrored in inland waters.

63. Stewart Dam: Natural freshwater lakes and ponds are rare on Prince Edward Island. In early days, many streams were dammed to provide waterpower for sawmills and gristmills. Today great care is being taken to provide fish ladders and yet prevent salt water from entering ponds leaving fresh water above a dam and salt below.

64. Whether as a diving platform or as a spot to quietly dangle hook and line, the wharves and the boats are second home for youngsters born and raised by the sea.

65. The need for working horses has been severely reduced, yet the animal is much loved, so much that there seems to be one at every turn. As the tide recedes, the wily racoon quickly searches for a favorite food, shellfish. Abandoned farm implements are a reminder of the era before mechanized agriculture. Lobster traps which have broken free of trap lines and washed ashore delight the beachcomber.

66. North Rustico: In days past all lighthouses were manned with living quarters close by or attached to the lighthouse. Today of the more than 60 wooden lighthouses in the province, only four are manned.

67. & 68. Wood Islands East: Small ponds and lakes provide a beautiful miniature water world, a delight for the birdwatcher, fly fisherman, canoeist and nature lover.

69. Located in Confederation Plaza at the foot of University Avenue the Cenotaph honors the high quota of Islanders who joined the fighting services in times of war. A large continent of volunteers went overseas in the South African War and by 1942, twelve per cent of the Island population had enlisted.

70. The former Law Court Building in Charlottetown, constructed between 1874 and 1876, and gutted by fire in 1976, has been renovated to house legislative offices and the Provincial Archives. Renamed the Hon. George Coles Building it honours the memory of the first premier who "set a worthy standard for all who follow."

71. Confederation Centre of the Arts in Charlottetown was opened in 1964 to celebrate the centenary of the Charlottetown Conference. It was designed to complement the historic legislative building next door. Its Art Gallery and Museum, considered to be among Canada's top five, houses a permanent collection of Canadian fine art and crafts, including the Robert Harris collection. The theatre is the focus of the annual Charlottetown Festival whose most known production, "Anne Of Green Gables", has been playing each summer since 1965.

72. Charlottetown Driving Park.

73. & 74. The "Birthplace of Confederation", Province House in Charlottetown was the site of the first conference of delegates to consider a Canadian Confederation in September, 1864. Built between 1843 and 1846 by Island craftsmen, designed by an Island architect, it was formerly known as the Colonial Building. Province House has been carefully restored; and is now a National Historic Site as well as the seat of the Provincial Legislature. The Confederation Chamber, re-created to its historical elegance, a theatre and exhibits are open to the public year round. Province House retains its position of grace and importance, sharing what was Queens Square (now known as Confederation Plaza) with the Coles Building and Confederation Centre of the Arts.

75. Charlottetown Driving Park: Not all the spectators are in the stands.

76. Island farmers become artists with their tractor and plough creating wonderful mosaics to be especially valued for their short life span.

77. Well kept dairy herds signify a healthy segment of the agricultural industry.

78. Clam digging, bathing in salt water and building sand castles are all part of an Island day "at the shore".

79. North Cape: Keeping a lonely sentinel... the lighthouse is an invaluable aid to mariners guiding their way at night, through fog and snow, and in rough weather. They warn of dangerous points of land, rocks, reefs, sandbars, and identify the locality as each light in a particular area has its own colour and characteristics, or flash pattern.

80. A combination of ocean currents, wind, geology and vegetation has given rise to the sand dunes of the north shore. Marram Grass, the dominant vegetation has a mass of tangled roots which help keep the sand in place. Without this "sand lover" the dunes would soon disappear and leave the coast unprotected. The sea would then move inland until a new equilibrium was established.

81. & 82. The spectacular coastal scenery is constantly being changed by the forces of wind, wave, winter ice, not to mention salt spray. These erosive forces continually grind away the shoreline sculpting ever new sand formations and red sand-stone cliff faces. The famous Cavendish cliffs in the National Park, unprotected, erode at a rapid pace — up to 5 metres per year.

83. Rounding a point in the headland will bring yet another panorama for those who take time to savour Prince Edward Island.

LLOYD OLIVER
P.E.I. DECOYS

10 1

GRANTS COUNTRY HOME

100

13

6374
ISLAND MORN
PRINCESS NOVA

6 17

SEA QUEEN II

STELLA MARIS I

The Old Mill
a museum with a difference
Hundreds Of Interesting
Educational AND Amusing Items
"A LOOK INTO THE PAST"..!
BUILT IN
1820
OPEN

27 28

BEVERLY MAC II
CHTOWN P.E.I.
WHITE FURY
CHARLOTTETOWN
P.E.I.

DEEP SEA
FISHING

CLEARANCE 13 6

COLES' DEEP SEA FISHING
L.M. MONTGO
BIRTHPLACE
MALPEQUE GARDEN
MALPEQUE GARDENS
MAGNETIC HILL
WOODLEIGH REPLICAS
Santa's WILDLIFE and WATER SLIDES
The OLD MILL Museum
Royal Atlantic WAX MUSEUM
Anne of GREEN GABLES MUSEUM
NEW LONDON LOBSTER SUPPERS
IRVI

WATERLOO
BARRACKS

OPEN
Lily's
OPEN

Autocar

7 58

59 60

THE SWAMP
KARL & SYLVIA
1-207-778-3172
7.
Ontario Fruit

FEDERATION
CONFEDERATION
LE THÉATRE DU
RE DE LA CONFÉD
BOX OFFICE
COURTYARD RESTAURANT
THE CHARLOTT
Anne
of Green Gables
MON.
8 PM

STEAD
ABLES

Glengyle Farm
LARIAT
BFGoodr

81 82